Schaum Generations

John W. Schaum
Originals
Level 3

Foreword by Wesley Schaum

My father, John W. Schaum, in addition to his widely-used "Schaum Piano Course" and "Note Speller," was probably best known for his skillful arrangements and transcriptions of music by a veritable Who's Who of composers, as well as folk songs and music of many genres.

Lesser known, perhaps, are his original compositions which span many levels and styles, a few of which have lyrics. The lyrics for "Pollution Solution," included in this book, are as relevant today as when originally written. His carefully chosen titles for all pieces remain both appropriate and charming.

The selections here for Level Three are compiled from various albums and sheet music published over the years. You will find they have retained their appeal and motivation for students.

INDEX

Armadillo Polka	10
Beach Ball Boogie	8
Bird Songs	13
Circus Capers	4
Glass Bottom Boat	2
Pollution Solution	14
Ship Ahoy	6
Squirrels in the Park	7
Stage Coach	3
Weeping Willow	16

Schaum Publications, Inc. • 10235 N. Port Washington Rd. • Mequon, WI 53092
www.schaumpiano.net

© Copyright 2014 by Schaum Publications, Inc., Mequon, Wisconsin
International Copyright Secured • All Rights Reserved • Printed in U.S.A.
ISBN-13: 978-1-62906-024-8

Warning: The reproduction of any part of this publication without prior written consent of Schaum Publications, Inc. is prohibited by U.S. Copyright Law and subject to penalty. This prohibition includes all forms of printed media (including any method of photocopy), all forms of electronic media (including computer images), all forms of film media (including filmstrips, transparencies, slides and movies), all forms of sound recordings (including cassette tapes and compact disks), and all forms of video media (including video tapes and DVD).

Glass Bottom Boat

John W. Schaum

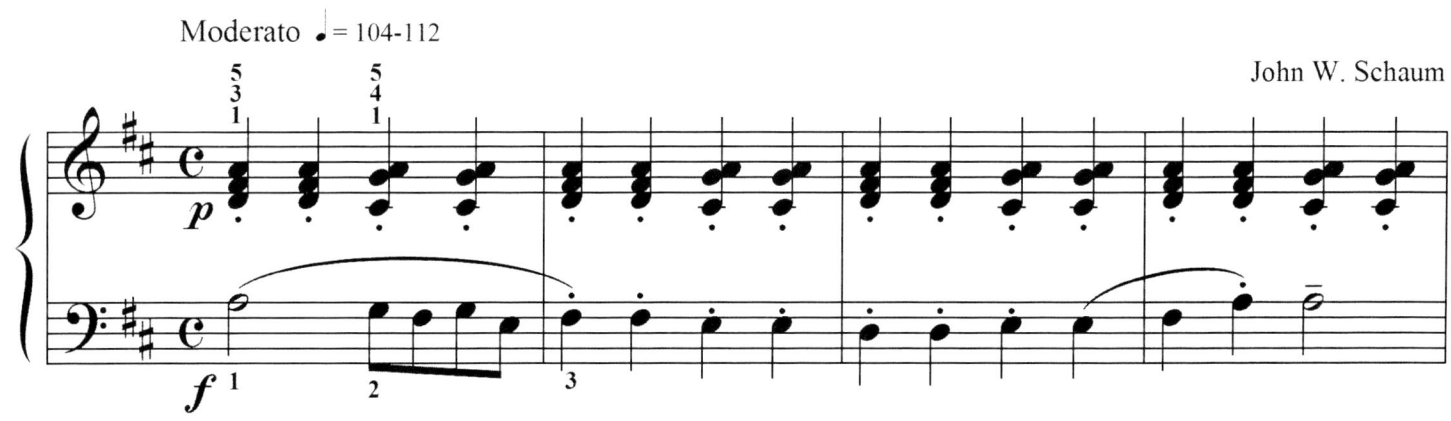

Teacher's Note: Explain the different dynamics for the treble accompanimnent and the bass melody.

Stage Coach

John W. Schaum

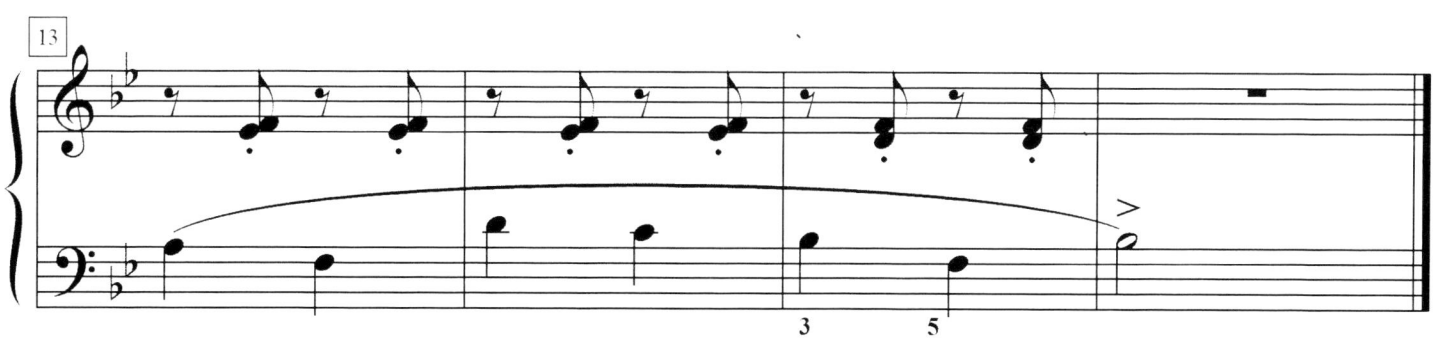

Circus Capers

John W. Schaum

(Play bass clef notes one octave lower than written.)

Capers are playful events with jumps and hops.

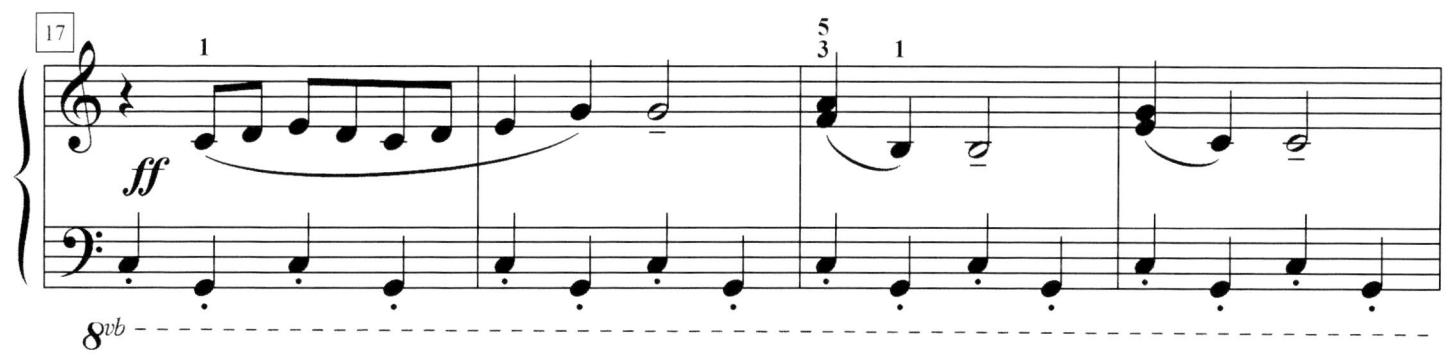
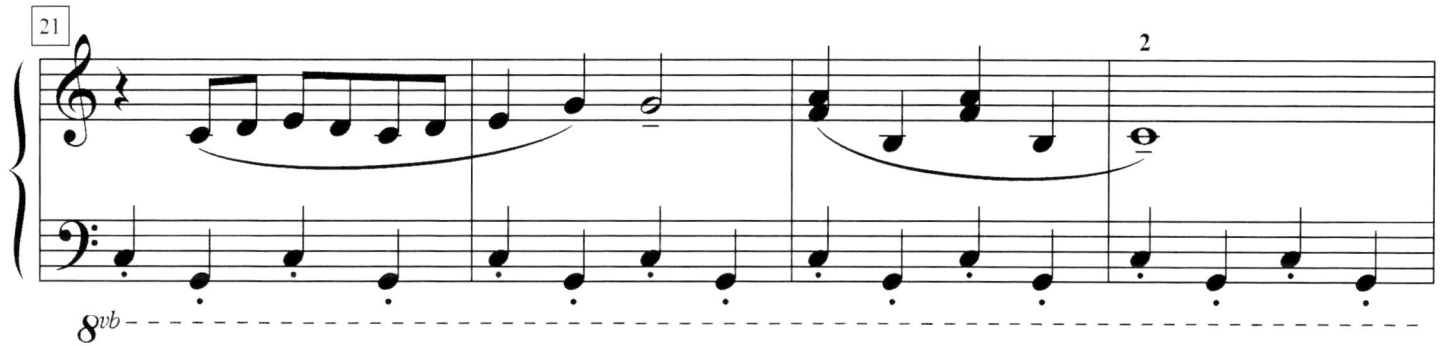

Ship Ahoy

John W. Schaum

Ahoy is an expression called out by sailors to greet or get the attention of someone within shouting distance.

Squirrels in the Park

John W. Schaum

Beach Ball Boogie

Allegretto ♩ = 100-108 *(swing 8ths)*

John W. Schaum

Teacher's Note: It may be necessary to explain "swing 8th notes" to the student.

* There is purposely no specific dynamic between these marks: <   > throughout the piece. The amount of increase and decrease is left to the discretion of the performer.

Armadillo Polka

John W. Schaum

An *armadillo* is an animal covered with hinged bony plates that overlap for armored protection.

Bird Songs

John W. Schaum

Teacher's Note: This piece has *measured trills* (with specific note values and number of notes) which are written out in measures 1 and 7. In other measures with the trill symbol, the trill should be played the same, using 16th note patterns and white keys.

Pollution Solution

Weeping Willow

Cantabile ♩. = 63-69

John W. Schaum